Mystical Nature

Sharada Muralidharan

ISBN

Paperback 979-8-89699-916-4
Hardcase 979-8-89744-650-6

I would like thank my friends and family who have been
with me through this journey, and have helped
me complete these poems!

My special thanks to my husband, who patiently read my
poems and gave his review. I would like to thank my daughter,
son and grandchildren for being my cheerleaders. I truly
appreciate my sister for her continuous encouragement.

I would like to dedicate this book to my parents who
were my guiding light.

Sharada

Contents

Break of Dawn

Glorious ray! you usher in dawn!

I wake up with a mighty yawn,

In awe I watch the sketch you have drawn,

Wow! In magnificent Orange and fawn!

Glorious ray you are the break of dawn!!

Oh gentle ray!!

You have opened up a wonderful day!

I see your portrait in a colorful display!

Fold my hands, unto to thee I pray,

Remove my darkness and the gray!!

Glorious ray you are the break of dawn!!

Oh you the mellow ray!!

You gently climb up the path that is high!

Your mighty beams spread without a sigh!

The dismal gloom around you defy,

Brightness and energy you never deny!

Glorious ray you are the break of dawn!

Oh placid ray!!

Your exuberance kindles my spirit,

Your splendor rejuvenates my form,

Your mighty beams strikes my soul,

I am ready to sing, dance and extol!

Glorious ray you are the break of dawn!

Great Egret!!

Look at those pristine white shiny plumes!
Wetlands and waterways are where you bloom!
Looking for your congregation...., I presume....,
Many a time above me you vroom.

Deep darkness surrounds you like night!
You ever shine snowy bright!
Neck shaped in S, you stand tall and tight.
Yellow dragger bills ready for a bite!

Grooming your quills in the mirror, under your feet?
Gazing at you is such a great treat!
I hear your raspy, nasal greet,
Glossy white wader, you look perfectly neat!

You are a symbol of spiritual peace!
Ever in a state of balance at ease,
Tranquility and gentleness you teach.
Watching you, flawless bird, serenity I reach.....!!

❧

Herons!!

Peck, peck, peck....
A dozen in all, eleven draped in white,
just one in misty gray!I
Immersed in looking for prey....???
Enthralled by your camaraderie all day.
Stately birds roost together in colonies.
Gentleness and grace are your exceptionalities!
Amazed to see your multiracial families!!
Statuesque birds, together form a pretty bouquet!
In unison you learn how to fly and play!
Solidarity and harmony is the message you relay!!

❧

Glorious Sky!!

What do I see in the sky so high?
Are they strawberry cream pie?
Or blueberry cheesecake floating by?
A perfect concoction of confection in the sky!!

Are these icing on the cupcake ?
Or a mighty cotton candy on the make,
May be a cream puff out of the bake,
What an amazing day break!!

We are awakened for the grand banquet!
Meticulously made to please our palate,
Delicately served on a golden platter!!
What a brilliant day starter!

These holy flowers sprinkled to welcome dawn?
What an exceptional fresh, fragrant, morn!
Love the magnificent floral pattern drawn....
Oh! Another spectacular day is born!!

Crack of Dawn!!

Few brilliant strokes is all it takes,

For a fabulous day break!

Spectacular array of color concoction you paint...!!

What a magnificent celestial tapestry you make!!

Amazing colors you mix and match,

To set the sky ablaze!

Magical flames that emanate, let the darkness raze!

Oh my ! the spectacle spawn, bids us to stand and gaze!

Gallons of vibrant colors you pour,

Makes our little hearts soar,

Dear lord, your lavish tints, we truly adore....!

Heavenly painter! We yearn to see your artistry ever more!

❦

Glorious Day

Oh! Another Glorious Day!!
Blue canvas with strokes of orange and gray!
Rising sun! a start to another gorgeous day!
Nature's art at play!!

Words can't describe your Splendor!!
Thy glory reflects on ponds and river,
Your grandeur is framed in gold and silver,
For all the magnificence you deliver!!!

You raise to remove the darkness,
And fill our spirits with a heavenly bliss!
It's time to thank and say....
Please help me rise and shine each day!
Oh! Another Glorious day!!

Hey Bird! Oh Bird!

What are you looking for...?

A meal or just enjoying the feel...?

Liking some solitude or Loving the altitude?

Hey bird, I'm just intrigued by your attitude!

Is this your entertainment, or your retirement!

Oh bird! You Bird!

You inspire me, you magnificent!

To take a break, and gaze ....(at)

Nature that is gorgeously chaste,

I'm dazzled by the glory,

My little eyes turn blurry...

Oh bird! Big bird!

Seasons change, years roll by,

There will come a time....

to say goodbye , good days!!

But, never too late to stand and stare......

Nature's beauty is Claire!!!

Oh bird, you bird!

Rainbow Fountain

I have seen you high up in the sky,
Never seen your color spectrum nearby!
The fountain glowed in the midday sun,
You made my heart leap up with fun!

VIBGYOR are the colors that shone bright,
Watching the spectacle was a pure delight!!
Gentle breeze rocked you to and fro,
It was magical to watch you glow!

As I moved away from your vicinity,
I see the colors blend into a unity
So.....clear, and so white, in purity!
Watching the show was a sheer ecstasy!

Sandhills Crane

Gray giants, you stand straight and tall,
Red head, white cheeks and all,
Wearing your soft gray overall!
You blow your trumpets to call!

Seen you by the clear pond,
Seeds, plants and insects, your fond,
Skillful dance, allures partner to respond!
Paired for life, what a bond!

You swoop from above flapping mighty wings,
Make a perfect landing with your limbs!
So agile, lithe, slim and trim...
It is a delight to watch you, as daylight dims...!

Stunning Twilight!

Sun is ready to set,

Sky lit up, looks its best,

Sundown, end to day's fest!

Flora and fauna are ready to rest!

The daylight fades, ring in twilight,

Cosmos is stunning, ravishing and bright!

Dusk awaits a streak of silverlight,

Moonlit night! Sure a fulsome sight!

Dressed in Orange, blue and gray,

For the Final show of the day,

Darkness is not here to stay,

Dawn will soon be on its way!

Tranquil River

Perfectly still, without a ripple,
As daybreak begins to sparkle,
The golden hue on the water is a marvel!
Peace permeates as we take an amble!

Fragrance of Oleanders fills the air,
Reeds awaked by the golden glare,
River glistens in its shiny wear!
Beauty at its zenith, makes us stare!

Banks hold the river in place,
Gives a direction to its maze.
Tranquil water's golden glaze,
Set the scene fair and ablaze!!

Burst of Colors!!!

Blue canvas hangs above our heads,
Strokes of Orange, yellow and red,
Magnificent glory, in a spread!
Await, to see more strokes ahead!!

Glory of the canvas mirrored below,
Water dazzles, shines, and glows!
Colorful ripples exalts the show,
As gentle breeze begins to blow.

Birth of a new day is around,
Burst of colors surround,
Shimmer and sheen abound!
Joy and bliss seem so profound...!

Mighty Brilliance

The stars have gone to sleep,
Moon has moved down to the deep,
Birds begin their tweets and cheep!
Clock awakens us with a beep!

Sunup sets the cosmos ablaze,
Sky glows with a tangerine glaze,
Glorious shades of heavenly haze.
As the golden ball begins to rise!

Magnificent brilliance engulfs the air,
Trees up, gently plays it's fanfare,
Ushers the amber gloss to change its wear,
What a stellar day in making, to share!!

Daybreak!

A Mesmerizing sight!
Amber light illuminates the ether,
Gives the daybreak's teaser,
Cosmos ready to open up its treasure,
Watching the presentation is sheer pleasure!!

Fields of Marigold in display,
Carpets of Primroses hail a new day!
Flocks of Goldfinch show at play,
Arcadian light bids adieu to gray!

Heaven sprayed in ocher delight!
Declares the end of a restful night.
Glow ball, ready, set to alight,
Truly a mesmerizing sight!

Reflection

Nature's beauty at its ace,
Reflecting poise and grace!
A scene to marvel and gaze,
Brings joy and smiles to our face!

Giant green trees form a lace,
Still waters watch them in praise!
The rising sun forms a silvery glacé,
Oh, my what a perfect place!!

The hush and stillness so divine,
Glory of dawn radiates and shines!
Blue waters, and sky well defined,
Lush trees paint a stunning design!!

Pure silence and lull just captivates,
Serenity and repose... resonates!
Sheer music of birds vibrates,
A glorious adobe to meditate!!

Divine Radiance

Heavenly refulgence rises in a mystical design,
The light of hope and wisdom ready to shine,
Cloud of ignorance and callowness decline,
Divine radiance seen from the celestial shrine!

Sparkling jewel on the crest,
String of diamonds look its best,
Aura of divinity fills the set,
Behold the magnificence, be Blessed!!

A Celestial Treat!

Pageantry begins as sun retreats,
Warm night unveils a celestial treat,
Magnificent glow seen in the East,
Mirrored on the river, oh so neat!

Mystic light illuminates the night,
Riverbed forms an aesthetic sight,
Aura of silence at its height!
A glimpse of glory, a pure delight!

River bank laced with reeds and trees,
Hails the heavenly luminary at ease,
Still water dazzles,without a crease,
Creates an ambience of serenity and peace!!

Dazzling Roseate!!

Never seen this beauty before,
Looking for dinner on the stream floor!
Emerald green grass adores the shore,
Your roseate plums, I sure adore!!

Where are the birds in your bowl?
Waiting for your mates in a knoll?
Or enjoying a solitary stroll....?
Your purity and grace refreshes our soul!

Spoonbill ready to sweep for prey?
Your Pearly quills glisten all day!
Neck so long, moves in a gentle sway!
Bewitching bird you take our breath away!!

A Magical Day Break!

Magnificent break of dawn!

Picturesque mix of colors shone,

What a brilliant tapestry drawn!

Birth of a fascinating morn!!

An amazing colorful spread,

Of yellow, orange and red,

Woven delicately in silken thread(s)

Welcome to a vivid day ahead!

Tints and tones seldom seen!

Yeah aurora, where have you been!

Trees lined up waiting to turn green!

Magical scene is so tranquil and serene!!

Feathery Clouds!!

Alabastrine birds on flight?!
Flapping their wings at a height..?
The show, a gazer's delight,
Truly a sublime sight!

Blue canopy spans above us,
Gentle wind blows in a quiet hush,
Friends in plumes seem in no rush!
Drifting above the meadows lush!

Feathery clouds ...? oh so neat!
In a tango to the celestial beat?
Never seen this heavenly feast,
A clear bright day's perfect treat!

Master's Orchestra!!

Sun up, time to buckle up in the East,
Sun down, time to unwind in the West,
Cosmos is never swathed in darkness,
This is the Creator's graciousness!!

Rooster trumpets, at first light.
Mockingbird croon, by moonlight.
Dawn awakens, each one's delight,
Night is dark, yet twinkles bright!

Nature is cyclical, always in motion,
Day, night and seasons change in precision.
Master's orchestra plays in unison!
This is the magnificence of evolution!

Silvery Moon!

Silvery moon to wane in the sky,
Larks and thrushes ready to fly!
Wake up! No time to ease and lie.
Rhythm of nature, no one can defy!

Inky clouds starts to glint and glow,
Setting stage for creator's next show!
Mistral winds awakens every bough,
As the Glistening moon sets sail to go... !

Glorious scene so tranquil and pure,
Sun begins its rise in the eastern pier,
Mist and fog are set to clear....
A spellbinding spectacle for sure!

June Moon

Mystical golden disk hangs high,
Its glory awes every passerby!
An exquisite heavenly jewel! Oh my!
A magnificent marvel in the sky!

Strawberry moon bids adieu to Spring,
Songbirds tune their cords to sing!
Wild berries ripen and gently swing,
June moon makes the high tide zing!

Lunar show at its zenith,
Heavenly glow, oh so mammoth!
Brilliant Cosmic halo seen beneath,
Heralds vibrancy, bliss,and growth!

Morning Beauty

Pink beauty stands gloriously bright!
Gently blooms at the first light!
A charmer, what an enthralling sight!
Blush blossoms, a sheer delight!

Studded with crystal drops of dew,
Allurer! you create an enticing view!
Swaying cheerfully as the warm breeze blew!
Your majestic poise mesmerizing woo!

Queen of Flowers!

Glorious, divine crimson bloom!
Spreads fresh fragrance in June,
Heart sings a sensuous tune,
Awaiting the sunny days soon!

Showers have bathed you fresh,
Adding sparkle to your vibrant dress,
See you quiver as the wind caress,
Hi velvety rose! you are our destress!

Stem slender, green and thorny,
Glossy leaves, margins so toothy,
Dazzling blooms,a colorful symphony
Symbol of love, joy and harmony!

Great Blue Heron

Hi stately bird! So majestic and tall!
Waiting for your partner's call?
Slaty plumes, pointy bill, you enthrall!
What poise and grit! A big applaud!

Standing by a creek at dawn,
Waiting for your catch this morn?
Slender legs pitched on the lawn,
Hey bird! You'll find a meal ,hang on!

Mighty, spiritual blue beauty!
A symbol of wisdom and tranquility,
Teaches power of stillness and humility,
Omen of good luck and prosperity!

Divine Rays

Divine effulgence of dawn,
Luminous day of hope born!
Darkness away, light beams shone,
Time to awake, and flex your brawn.

Rays of life illuminates the sky,
New beginning rings from heaven high!
Close of duskiness, murk and gloom,
Get set for tabula rasa to loom!

Blue Bird's Bootie

Hi, Magnificent dusky beauty,
Standing by the creek, too sooty,
Spotted your day break's bootie?!
Oh so agile, big birdie!

Out for a nosh by the crack of dawn?
Darkness of the night is gone,
Gold hued creek dazzled and shone!
Spied your chow by the spawn..?

Super Blue Moon!

A magical night in the making!
Magnificent and breathtaking!
Brilliant glow! simply striking!
A scene, dazzling and electrifying!

Oh silvery moon! so enormous!
Luminaries sing thy praise in chorus!
Bejeweled Luna! stunning and gorgeous!
A Cosmic event, serenely picturesque!

Curtains open for a night show,
Super moon to perform a solo!
Glam , glitter, moon's awesome halo!
Lustrous display, so tranquil and mellow!

Saffron West!

Oh ! Look at the grandeur of sunset!
Divine artist paints a saffron west!
Sprays an inky blue, gray east!
Master tints the sky to look it's best !

The mystical canvas radiates a glow,
Creator blends hues in a free flow!
Tones and shade yet so Mellow,
Ornate sky shines for folks below!

Twilight ushers tranquil transition,
Dusk brings a colorful celebration!
Cosmos is ready for an illumination!
Wish for nothing, but a peaceful salvation!

Who is the Artist? Any Clue?

Heavenly Strokes of amber and blue!
Canvas brushed in glorious hue!
Colors dazzle in each silvery dew!
Who is the artist? Any clue..?

Rays of grandeur sprayed above,
Artist's designs, we just adore!
Tints, tones, and stains abound,
Who is the artist? Any clue?

Maestro styles cosmos each morn!
Coral, salmon,tangerine and fawn!
Oh my! Spectacular shades of dawn!
Who is the Artist? Any clue?

Each brush stroke is our inspiration,
Creator's productions, a celebration!
We bow to thee for your creations!
HE is the Artist! Got your clue!?

Goodbye Moon!

Goodbye moon, goodbye night,
Luna! Kept dusk radiant and bright,
Flashing its brilliant lustrous light!
Adieu,as it slowly fades out of sight!

Dawn opens a bright blue curtain,
The drowsy trees, leisurely awaken,
To melodies of song birds beckon,
A perfect day in making, for certain!

Mystical silence engulfs the air,
Tranquility and repose begin to pair,
New day crafted with love and care!
A blessing created for us to share!